GROW IT
COOK IT

LONDON, NEW YORK,
MELBOURNE, MUNICH, and DELHI

Senior designer Sonia Whillock-Moore
Senior editor Deborah Lock
Designers Sadie Thomas, Rachael Smith,
Gemma Fletcher
US editor Margaret Parrish
Photography Will Heap
Food stylist Annie Nichols
RHS consultant Simon Maughan
Food consultant Jill Bloomfield

Category publisher Mary Ling
Production editor Clare McLean
Production controller Claire Pearson
Jacket designers Sonia Moore, Sadie Thomas
Jacket editor Mariza O'Keeffe
Jacket copywriter Adam Powley

First published in the United States in 2008 by DK Publishing
375 Hudson Street, New York, New York 10014
Foreword copyright © 2008 Jill Bloomfield
Copyright © 2008 Dorling Kindersley Limited
08 09 10 11 12 10 9 8 7 6 5 4 3 2 1
GD103 – 02/08

A catalog record for this book is available from
the Library of Congress
ISBN 978-0-7566-3367-7

Color reproduction by MDP, UK
Printed and bound by TBB, Slovakia

Discover more at
www.dk.com

Contents

Foreword

Growing your own fruits and vegetables is easy and fun. Imagine growing a pumpkin of your very own or a bunch of bright orange carrots. With tending and patience, a seed you sow will become a tiny green seedling poking out of the dirt. By watering and feeding your plant, it will become strong and bear blossoms and leaves. The plant will bud tiny fruits or vegetables that will grow bigger and bigger before your eyes. Imagine how fun harvesting your fruits and vegetables will be! You might have lots of juicy tomatoes, sweet strawberries, or shiny eggplants.

You can share your harvest with others by cooking these yummy recipes. Eating blueberry cheesecake in summer and pumpkin pies in fall reminds us that the freshest, healthiest, and tastiest food is grown right in your own garden! So, get ready to plan your plot to grow the amazing ingredients you need to cook up a feast for family and friends.

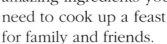

Know it Green-thumbed gardener

Whatever you decide to grow, caring for your plants is the key to becoming a "green-thumbed" gardener. Thinking about what your plants need will help you choose what tools and equipment you need to have.

Remember to wear old clothes because you'll be getting your hands dirty! You'll also need boots or shoes that you can get dirty.

Trial and error is the way many gardeners learn. Finding out what works and what doesn't is part of the fun of gardening.

Light

Plants need the Sun's warmth but also protection from wind and rain. Find suitable places for growing your plants inside and outside. You need pots and containers or a small garden patch to grow your plants in. See page 6.

Grow it symbols

A sunny or slightly shaded place

A warm, sheltered, sunny place

A place with direct sunlight

Soil

Plants need good soil that provides grip for the roots, prevents water from draining away, and is filled with nutrients (goodness) for healthy growing. You need a hand trowel, hand fork, and a small rake for preparing the soil for the plants. A wheelbarrow is useful, too.

Compost adds goodness to the soil.

See page 14 for tips on how to make your own rich, crumbly compost.

Water

Plants need water to make their food, but some plants need less water than others. Water in the soil is drawn up by the roots and transported to the leaves through the stem. Also, spraying some plants with water helps their fruit to set. You need a watering can and a spray bottle.

Support

Some plants need support as they grow tall, since their stems have to support the weight of the fruit. You need poles and twine.

Cover the top of your pole to protect your eyes.

Support your large fruit in hammocks made from the netting of an orange bag.

Protection

Plants need to be protected from some garden bugs and diseases. There are many creatures that eat the pests, such as birds and ladybugs, which eat aphids. Strong-scented herbs may drive away any pests with their smell. Also try companion planting—see pages 19 and 45.

Protect young plants from hungry slugs and snails by putting them on a tabletop. Use eggshells around the plants as well.

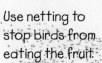

Use netting to stop birds from eating the fruit.

You'll need pots and containers in all shapes and sizes, depending on what plants you decide to grow, and for keeping them healthy throughout their growing stages.

Small pots

Small pots for sowing seeds need to be between 2 in (5 in) and 3 in (7.5 cm) deep in size. Start a collection of yogurt and dessert cups and tubs. They can all be reused as pots.

Pots and more pots
Transform your balcony or patio by growing plants in an array of pots of all shapes, sizes, and colors.

Ice-pop sticks can be used as labels

Empty yogurt pots that have been washed out well

Biodegradable egg cartons that will rot away when put directly into soil

Empty dessert cups

A plastic egg carton can become a mini greenhouse

Odd pots

Reuse ice cream tubs to plant seeds; use lids as drip trays.

Cut off the top of a large plastic container and it becomes a pot.

To prepare the small pots, ask an adult to make a couple of holes in the bottom for drainage, using a pair of scissors or something similar with a sharp point. Fill the pot with rich seedling potting soil ready to sow your seeds.

Large pots

Medium pots between 5 in (12 cm) and 6 in (15 cm) across are needed for transplanting seedlings that have outgrown their sowing pot but are not yet ready to be kept outside all the time.

You will also need long containers about 12 in (30 cm) long and large containers between 8 in (20 cm) to 14 in (35 cm) across.

Potatoes in tires

A laundry basket, old boots, or even an old drawer are some of the unusual ideas for a plant container. Line them with a waterproof plastic sheet, punch out a few small holes, and they're ready to use.

If you have the space, you could grow your plants in your own yard. Make a small raised bed so that you don't step on the soil to get to your plants.

Preparing pots

⚠

1 **Ask an adult** to make some holes in the bottom of the container if there are none.

2 **Place some crock** (pieces of broken pots) or some large stones over the holes. These will prevent the soil from draining away through the holes when you are watering the plants.

3 **Fill the container** with rich soil ready for a plant.

Some vegetables and fruits have many varieties, which means each one will be different. Look out for the variety on the seed packet and include it on your label.

As you plant your seeds, remember to add a label. When seedlings appear, it can get very confusing to identify which plant is which. Your labels can be as simple as writing on ice-pop sticks, or you can have some fun making and decorating your own.

Stone markers

Mark the pots that you have used with colorful stones. What eye-catching designs will you paint?

Maybe paint a stone in one color and then choose another color for a flower or the first letter of your name.

Paint

Tall labels

Labels on sticks will stand out in a pot. They are ideal markers for plants that will grow tall and bushy, such as herbs. Waterproof labels can be made using pizza bases, which are also easy to cut and paint.

You will need:

skewers

Recycle a pizza base

Reuse an old plastic bottle

1. Carefully cut off the base of your bottle.

2. Cut a small circle out of your pizza base.

3. Push your skewer inside the circle and glue to the bottle base.

Basil

Now decorate your flower.

Keep a record of what label you have used for which plant.

Butterfly

1. Draw a butterfly on a pizza base. Cut it out.

2. Push your skewer inside the butterfly. Now it's ready to paint.

Ice-pop stick labels

Ice-pop sticks are very handy as labels for small seed pots. Use pens to draw a picture of the vegetable you have planted or to make a striped pattern in the same shades of color as the vegetable.

You can also use a clothes pin to label your seedling.

Paint the end of a ice-pop stick to measure how deep to make your seed hole.

$1/3$ in (1 cm)

1 in (2 cm)

$1 1/3$ in (3 cm)

Leek

9

As a gardener, you will be taking care of your plants throughout their life cycles. The growth of a seed into a seedling is called **germination**. Seeds will start germinating if they have enough water, air, and warmth.

Seed leaves are the first ones to appear, but they look different from the plant's true leaves.

The seed contains all the food that the new plant needs to grow.

1 day +

2 days +

Seed leaves

Seed coat

Food store

Seed leaves

Seed roots

The true leaves form after the seed leaves. They have a distinctive shape and this will help you to identify the plant. With leaves, the seedling can now begin to make its own food and grow. This process is called **photosynthesis**. The leaves are where photosynthesis takes place.

For photosynthesis, plants take carbon dioxide [CO_2] from the air and water from the soil, and use sunlight to join them together to make sugar-based food. Oxygen [O_2] is released as a waste product and humans need this to breathe.

Sunlight

O_2

CO_2

Water

The stem supports the plant and transports water and nutrients from the roots to the leaves.

True leaves

Seed leaves

3-5 days +

A week +

Tomatoes, zucchinis, and blueberries are just some of the "fruits" of a plant that we eat. But how do plants form these and what can gardeners do to encourage their growth? The answer is found in the secret workings of flowers.

Insects, such as bees, get covered in pollen as they drink from the sweet nectar in the flower. The bee collects pollen on its back legs to take back to its hive.

Flowers are the place where the male and female parts of a plant are found. To form fruits, the male powdery yellow pollen has to reach the female ovules, which are like the eggs. This process is called **pollination.**

While some plants can self-pollinate, others need a little help from insects, animals, or the wind to move pollen around from flower to flower.

1 **This tomato plant** has bright yellow flowers for attracting insects. The bee is already covered in pollen from the last tomato flower it visited.

2 **Once the pollen grains** have rubbed off the bee onto the flower's stigma, they travel down to the ovary, or egg chamber, where the pollen enters the ovules. Then the fruit starts to grow and the yellow petals fall away.

When tomatoes were first brought to Europe from South America in the 1500s, people thought they were poisonous. Tomato-eating demonstrations were held in market places to prove that they were safe to eat.

3 Sunshine, water, and nutrients from the soil help the tomato to grow bigger and become firm. So keep watering and using a liquid plant food as required.

4 The fruit changes color and once it is red and ripe is ready for picking. Cut the fruit in half and you will see the seeds that the fleshy part has been protecting. The plant wilts and dies, but its seeds might survive to bring new life.

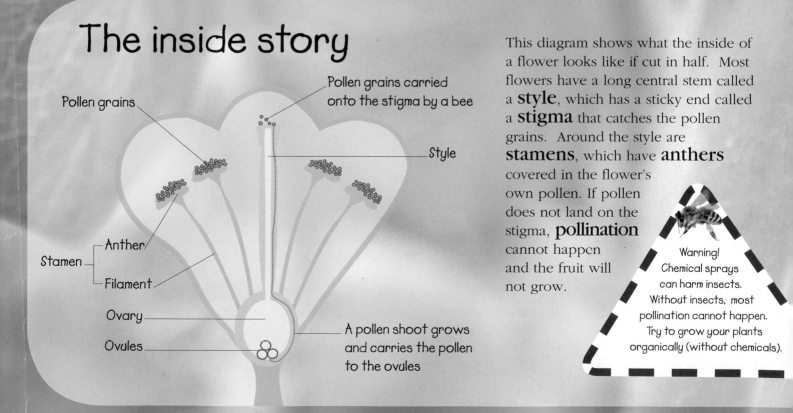

The inside story

Pollen grains

Pollen grains carried onto the stigma by a bee

Style

Stamen
— Anther
— Filament

Ovary

Ovules

A pollen shoot grows and carries the pollen to the ovules

This diagram shows what the inside of a flower looks like if cut in half. Most flowers have a long central stem called a **style**, which has a sticky end called a **stigma** that catches the pollen grains. Around the style are **stamens**, which have **anthers** covered in the flower's own pollen. If pollen does not land on the stigma, **pollination** cannot happen and the fruit will not grow.

Warning! Chemical sprays can harm insects. Without insects, most pollination cannot happen. Try to grow your plants organically (without chemicals).

What can you do with all your fruit and vegetable peelings, old plants, grass clippings, and fall leaves? You can use them to make wonderful, rich soil or layers of mulch for the plants you'll grow next year. The nutrients from these decaying plants can be recycled.

For this section, always let an adult help you and wear gardening gloves.

Making your own compost

One of the easiest ways of making compost if you have only a small space is to buy a plastic garbage can. By adding layer on layer of waste that will rot down inside the container, you'll have excellent, crumbly compost six to nine months later.

1 Choose a partly sunny site for composting. Place the container on dirt and not concrete, so that water can drain out and helpful bugs can get in.

2 Keep filling your compost heap with equal amounts of "green" and "brown" waste to get the best mix.

The "browns" are the tough, dry waste, such as scrunched paper, egg cartons, and leaves. They provide fiber and carbon and form air pockets for the bugs.

The "greens" are the young, wet waste, such as peelings, grass clippings, and teabags, that will rot quickly. They provide nitrogen and moisture.

3 Cover the container with a lid or an old piece of carpet or doormat to keep in the heat to encourage the bugs. Sprinkle in some soil and, every month or so, ask an adult to help you mix the top few layers with a gardening fork, so the waste will rot faster. You'll notice the heap rotting down and reducing in size. It will smell dirty!

Your plants will love this rich, dark compost.

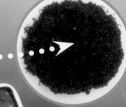

Don't put these in your compost:
Soot, cat litter, dog feces, disposable diapers, glossy magazines, cooked food, meat, oil, fish, newspapers.

Compost critters

Rich, crumbly compost is partly made up of bugs' very dark poop. So, you'll see many busy bugs living in your container. Some bugs feed on the green and brown organic waste you've put in. Others shred this waste and tunnel through it, mixing it up.

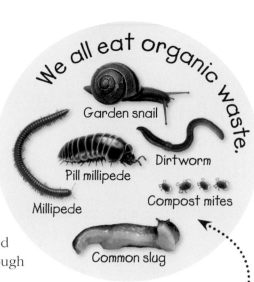

We all eat organic waste.

Garden snail
Dirtworm
Pill millipede
Compost mites
Millipede
Common slug

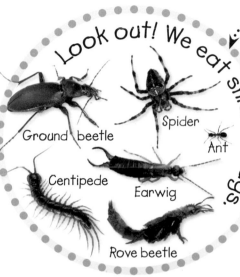

Look out! We eat smaller bugs.

Ground beetle
Spider
Ant
Centipede
Earwig
Rove beetle

If you have these, you'll get these!

The large numbers of these smaller, organic-eating bugs attract bigger bugs to the compost heap in search of food.

Make your own leaf mold

Punch a few holes in the side and bottom of a garbage-can liner. Gather up piles of fall leaves and put them in the bag. When the bag is almost full, sprinkle the leaves with water, then shake the bag and tie it up. Store it in a shady spot.

After a year, the leaves will have rotted down into a rich, crumbly mixture. Spread this over your soil, and your plants will thrive.

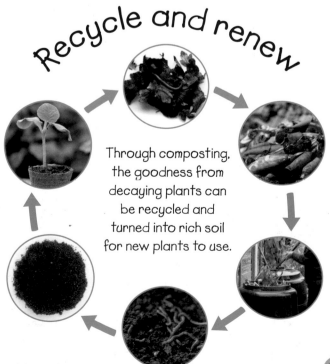

The magic of mulching

Another great gardening tip is to try out mulching. Mulch is a layer covering the surface of the soil that provides nutrients to the plants, keeps in the moisture, prevents weeds from growing, and helps to protect the roots from the cold. Some possible things to use are tree bark, pine needles, grass clippings, and even seaweed.

Recycled glass beads or seashells can be used as decorative mulch.

Recycle and renew

Through composting, the goodness from decaying plants can be recycled and turned into rich soil for new plants to use.

Cook it Kitchen know-how

Here's a list of useful cooking terms, with pictures showing what equipment you'll need when you make the recipes with your homegrown food.

 Preheat: Turn the oven on before you start following the recipe, so that the oven will have reached the right temperature when you are ready to bake.

 Ask an adult: It's necessary to be careful in the kitchen. Using knives, ovens, and stoves can cause harm, so ask an adult to help when you see this symbol in the recipes.

Grate: Cut an ingredient into small pieces by rubbing it up and down against the sides of a grater.

Drizzle: Pour a liquid slowly over the top of a dish.

Pour: Add a liquid ingredient or mixture into a bowl or pan.

Beat: Using a wooden spoon, quickly mix the ingredients around and around in a bowl to make a smooth mixture.

Stir: Mix the ingredients in a bowl very gently.

Whisk: Mix ingredients in a bowl very well with a whisk or electric mixer until the mixture is light, fluffy, and full of air.

Blend: Whiz ingredients together very quickly in a food processor or blender until it is impossible to tell one from another in the smooth mixture.

Knead: Handle dough by folding over and pressing down with the heel of your hand.

Roll out: On a lightly floured surface, flatten a ball of mixture to the right thickness, using a rolling pin dusted with flour.

Simmer: Cook a mixture in a saucepan over a low heat so that it bubbles very slowly.

Boil: Heat a mixture in a saucepan until it bubbles very quickly.

Stir-fry: Cook the ingredients in a wok or a frying pan on top of the stove.

Bake: Cook the mixture in the oven. The mixture can be in a muffin pan, on a cookie sheet, in a roasting pan, or some other heatproof container as mentioned in the recipe.

Fry: Cook the ingredients in hot oil in a frying pan on top of the stove.

Rub: Use your fingertips to rub fat and flour together, lifting them out of the bowl slightly, until the mixture looks like fine breadcrumbs.

Drain or strain: Pour a mixture into a strainer or colander to separate the liquid part from the solid part.

Tomato

Round or plum-shaped, cherry- or monster-sized, yellow, orange, green, striped, or just deep red, there are lots of tomato varieties to grow and try out. Which will be your favorite?

1 **Fill a shallow** container, with soil. Scatter the seeds thinly over the surface. Make sure the container has holes in the bottom for drainage.

2 **Cover the seeds** with a thin layer of soil, then water them gently. Add a label, then place the container on a windowsill.

3 **Thin out the seedlings** to allow room for others to continue growing and developing good roots. Water to keep the soil moist but not too wet.

4 **Once two true leaves** have formed, the seedlings are ready to be put into individual small pots. Be gentle and careful as you place in a seedling.

5 **Once your plant** has grown twice as high as its pot, plant it into a larger pot. Make a hole first, then place in the plant, pat the soil around it, and water.

Put a plastic bottle on the pole to cap the blunt end.

6 **Push** in a pole a little away from the main stem. Use string to tie the stem to the pole.

7 **Pinch out** the shoots that appear where the leaves join the stems. Pinch out the growing tip once your plant has four or five flowering stems, or "trusses."

8 **Fine-spray the plant** with water to encourage the fruits to set. Water each day and add liquid plant food every week to grow the best fruit.

Is a tomato a fruit or a vegetable? This depends on who you ask. Until the late 1800s, it was labeled as a fruit so people did not have to pay taxes when buying them.

Red and ripe, ready for picking!

Grow marigolds in the same pot as your tomato plant. These flowers can keep away aphids, which might otherwise infest your tomato plant. This is called companion planting.

Eggplant

An eggplant has not always been a dark purple fruit. It's evolved from a spiny plant with a small, white egg-shaped fruit from India. This is where the eggplant gets its name.

1 Fill a pot with potting soil after making some holes in its base (see page 6). With your fingertips, make a hole about ¼ in (6 mm) deep in the soil.

2 Sow two seeds in the hole and gently brush some surrounding soil over with your fingers. Remember to add a label and water. Keep on a windowsill.

3 After germinating, remove the weakest seedling to allow the strongest one to continue growing and developing good roots.

4 Make a hole in a large container. Carefully, tip the young plant out of its pot and place into the hole. Pat the soil around it and water.

5 Water little but often, since eggplants don't like their soil too wet or too dry. If you have a greenhouse, your plant will flourish if kept there.

6 Look for flowers. These have five petals with a yellow center. They are very colorful to attract the insects to the plant for pollinating.

7 **Spray with water** the new fruits that develop from the flowers. As the fruits start to swell, add liquid plant food each time you water.

8 **Pinch out** the growing tips once the plant has grown to 12 in (30 cm). You may wish to tie your plant to a stake for added support.

Cut each fruit with scissors when it is over 4 in (10 cm) long and still has a shine on its skin. You might get between five and 10 fruits over the next few months.

Cook it Tomato and eggplant towers

Eggplants and slow-roasted tomatoes are so easy to prepare and burst with flavor. They can be used in salads, soups, bruschetta, and sauces.

You'll need

| 6 large ripe tomatoes, cut in half | 2 garlic cloves, finely chopped | 1 tbsp dried oregano | 8 tbsp extra-virgin olive oil | sea salt and freshly ground black pepper | 1 large eggplant | pinch of smoked paprika | 8 tbsp of plain yogurt | 2 tbsp of honey | 4 tbsp roasted, blanched almonds | Preheat 300°F, 150°C |

thinly sliced

chopped roughly

1 Lay the tomatoes cut-side up on a cookie sheet. Mix the garlic and oregano with the salt, pepper, and half the olive oil. Spoon this over the tomatoes.

Baking time 3–4 hours

2 Bake in the oven. Check the tomatoes every now and then. When ready, they should be slightly shrunk, but still a brilliant red color. Allow to cool.

3 Layer the slices of eggplant in a colander, sprinkling a little salt between each layer. Leave for 30 minutes then rinse well with water and dry.

Tomatoes can be eaten right after picking. Go ahead, try one!

4 Place the eggplant slices in a large bowl, pour over the rest of the olive oil, and sprinkle with a little paprika. Toss together with your hands.

Cooking time 2–3 mins

5 Heat a ridged griddle pan and then add a single layer of the eggplant slices. Cook each side until tender. Place the slices on a plate. Repeat for the other slices.

Pour on some honey and sprinkle with chopped almonds.

Go to page 78 for more tomato and eggplant recipe ideas.

6 **To serve, create** towers by piling up the eggplant slices and tomato halves in alternate layers. Drizzle two tablespoons of yogurt over each tower.

Grow zucchinis in a sunny place, sheltered from the wind.

Zucchini
As a member of the squash family, the zucchini plant can grow very large. Each year, why not choose a different variety, since zucchinis can be many odd shapes, colors, and sizes?

1 **Push two seeds** on their sides down into a ½ in (1.5 cm) deep hole in a small pot filled with soil. Water well, label, and put the pot on a windowsill.

2 **Remove the weakest** seedling and put the strong one outside during the daytime. Cover the plant with part of a plastic bottle for protection.

3 **When the roots** begin to show through the bottom of the pot, the plant is ready to place into the ground or a big container. Dig out a hole.

5 **Look out** for the bright yellow male and female flowers. They open up to attract insects, which will pass pollen from the male to the female flowers.

6 **Water the soil** around the plant and not over the plant, since this could cause rotting. Keep the soil moist. Use a liquid plant food to encourage more fruit to grow.

7 **Pick off** the female flower from the tip of the growing zucchini. These can be cooked and eaten. If left on, they will shrivel and drop off by themselves.

Planting in pots

Zucchini plants will thrive in pots, especially if kept well fed and watered. You could bury a small pot into the soil next to your plant. Water into this, so the water flows to the roots of the plant.

4 Tip the young plant out of its pot, carefully supporting it at the base of its stem. Place it in the hole, fill gaps with soil, pat around it, and water.

8 Cut the zucchinis at their base when they reach 4 in (10 cm) long. Ask an adult to help, since a sharp knife needs to be used for cutting.

Zucchinis are young marrows, so you might choose to leave a few attached to grow twice as long to become large marrows.

Cook it Zucchini frittata

Ciao! This recipe is not just an ordinary omelet, but an Italian one filled with your homegrown vegetables. Buon appetito! (Have a good meal!)

1 lb (500 g) new potatoes

2 oz (50 g) butter

1 large onion, finely chopped

3 zucchinis, thinly sliced

1 tbsp fresh mint leaves, chopped

8 eggs

finely grated
3 oz (75 g) Pecorino cheese

pinch of ground black pepper

1 Cook the potatoes in boiling water for 15-20 minutes or until tender. Use a colander to drain them. Let them cool down, and then halve, if large.

Cooking time 5 mins

2 Melt the butter in a 10 in (28 cm) diameter, nonstick frying pan. Add the onion and cook gently until soft. Add the zucchinis and cook. Stir often.

Cooking time 5 mins

3 Stir in the potatoes and continue cooking for a further five minutes, until the zucchinis have softened.

4 Crack the eggs into a bowl and add the cheese and mint and season well with pepper. Whisk together well using a fork.

Cooking time 5 mins

5 Pour the egg mixture into the pan and turn the heat down as low as possible.

Cooking time 5 mins

6 When the eggs are just set, place the pan under a preheated broiler to brown the top. When ready, remove from the broiler and leave the frittata to cool.

A brilliant dish for picnics!

Go to page 78 for another zucchini recipe idea.

Pumpkin

These large, heavy fruits belong to the squash family. Pumpkins take a long time to ripen, but varieties of summer squash will grow quicker. The hard, inedible skins make these fruits ideal for storing for a while.

1 In spring, fill a pot with soil and make a ½ in (1.5 cm) deep hole. Sow one seed on its side into the hole, cover with soil, and water. Put on a windowsill.

2 Keep well watered after germination. Your plant will be ready to transplant once the roots begin to show through the bottom of the pot.

3 Make a pot-sized hole in a large, deep container. Carefully place the plant into the hole. Pat around the base to make sure the plant is upright. Water.

5 Keep the soil well watered. Your plant will produce male and female flowers, attracting insects to visit both to pollinate.

6 Feed your plant with suitable plant food every few weeks once the fruits start to form in the female flowers. The flowers will now shrivel and drop off.

7 Make a hammock out of netting to support any fruit growing above the ground. Attach the ends of the hammock to the poles.

Once it has reached 2 ft (60 cm), break off the growing tip so the plant can redirect goodness to its fruit.

Native Americans not only used pumpkins for savory and dessert dishes, but also used dried strips of pumpkin to weave into mats.

4 **Push four poles** into the pot and wrap the stem around them. Tie the stem to the poles with string. As the stem grows longer, continue to wrap it around the poles and tie up.

8 **Add mulch** around fruit growing on the ground to cushion it. Keep turning the fruit slightly so the color ripens evenly. The leaves will now start dying.

9 **Cut the fruit** once it has fully matured. Ask an adult to help you cut it and lift it.

Cook it Mini pumpkin pies

You'll need

Ask an adult to cut the pumpkin in half with a sharp knife, using a rocking motion. Scoop out the seeds. Slice the pumpkin into pieces, and cut off the peel.

peeled, deseeded		cut into 16 pieces								Preheat
1 lb (500 g) pumpkin, cut into large chunks	1 tbsp olive oil	1 lb (375 g) puff pastry	1 tbsp all-purpose flour	¼ cup (90 g) molasses	1 whole egg	3 large egg yolks	1½ cups (300 ml) milk	½ a split vanilla pod	a pinch of salt	375°F, 190°C

Roasting time
30–35 mins

1 **On a cookie sheet,** pour olive oil over the pumpkin pieces. Evenly coat them, using your hands. Roast until tender. Cool and then mash with a fork.

Refrigerate for 30 mins

2 **Shape the puff pastry** pieces into balls. Roll out each ball until about 2½ in (6 cm) in diameter. Press each piece into a muffin pan and put into the fridge.

Handy tip!

Baking time
15 mins

3 **Place a piece of** parchment paper into each pastry and fill to the top with baking beans. Bake in the oven then remove the paper and beans.

4 **Pour the milk** into a pan. Scrape out the vanilla seeds from the pod and add to the milk. Heat the mixture until just below boiling point. Leave to partly cool.

5 **Lightly beat** the egg yolks, whole egg, and molasses in a bowl. Add the flour and salt and beat until smooth. Strain the hot milk over the mixture and beat.

6 **Pour the smooth** mixture into a pan and bring to the boil, stirring all the time until thickened. Remove from heat and stir in the pumpkin puree.

Go to page 78 for another pumpkin recipe idea.

7 Spoon out the mixture evenly into the pastry shells. Bake in the oven for 20-25 minutes until just firm and slightly puffed up. Serve the pies warm with a dusting of confectioner's sugar on the top, if you wish.

Grow beans in a sunny, sheltered place.

Beans
Pole or French, long or dwarf, you'll have a tough choice deciding which beans to grow. You also have a choice about how to sow your beans. Here are two ways to get started.

Scarlet pole bean flower

Either, plant one bean seed per small pot, or a handful of beans around a large shallow container to get them started. Cover with soil, water, and label. Once the seedlings have grown their true leaves, transplant them to the base of a pole wigwam structure. Put one or two at the base of each pole.

1 Or, push four poles into a large pot and tie them together at the top to make a wigwam structure.

2 Press the beans about 2 in (5 cm) deep into the soil. Plant one on each side of a pole. Cover with soil and water. Write a label with the bean name.

3 Wind each seedling around its nearest pole, and then it will continue to grow up it. Cover the soil with straw or mulch and protect the plants from slugs.

4 Rub off any aphids you see with your fingers, or squirt them with a spray of water. Keep watering the soil often and use a liquid plant food every two weeks.

People have been
growing beans for many
thousands of years.
Since ancient times,
beans have been eaten
as a good source
of protein.

5 **Pick the beans**
when they are
long but still young
and tender. Pick
regularly so that
other beans will
grow. You could
get a crop for
the next eight
weeks.

Leave a few pods
on your plant to dry
out, so you can
open and reuse
the beans inside
to grow bean
plants next year.
See page 76.

🥘 Cook it Giant beanstalk stir-fry

Grab yourself a handful of beans from your beanstalk and be amazed at how quickly you can conjure up a stir-fry for any Giant's appetite!

You'll need

unsweetened				sliced	thinly sliced			chopped		½ cup (75 g) unsalted cashew nuts
½ cup (50 g) shredded coconut	2 tbsp sunflower oil	1 clove of garlic, sliced	6 spring onions, chopped	1 bulb of fennel (core taken out)	4 cups (500 g) green beans	2 tbsp soy sauce, 1 tbsp rice vinegar	1 cup (100 g) bean sprouts	2 tbsp cilantro	2 cup (200 g) wholewheat noodles	1 tbsp sesame seeds

1 Place the coconut in a bowl of warm water, cover, and leave for 20 minutes. Strain the coconut through a strainer, pressing it against the sides.

2 Heat the oil in a large frying pan or wok. Add the garlic, onion, and fennel. Stir all the time for about two minutes, using a wooden spoon.

3 Add your sliced beans and fry quickly, stirring all the time. Pour on the soy sauce and vinegar. Stir in, then remove the pan from the heat.

4 Add the bean sprouts to the stir-fry. Sprinkle on the coconut and cilantro. Then stir the mixture well for a second time. Mmm! Smells good.

5 Cook some noodles, following the instructions on the package. Drain the noodles using a strainer, then spoon them into your serving bowls.

6 Spoon out the stir-fry on top of the noodles. After roasting the cashew nuts and sesame seeds, sprinkle over and serve. Fee fi fo fum, here I come!

Go to page 78 for another bean recipe idea.

Crunchy, nutty beans

Potato

Slowly growing, hidden from view, potatoes are the enlarged parts of the underground stem of a potato plant. They are called "tubers." You can choose from a variety of potatoes; in the US, potatoes can be divided into four categories—russet, long white, round white, or round red.

1 **Buy seed potatoes** at the end of winter. Lay them out separately with their "eyes" uppermost in a cool, dry, light place or windowsill. They'll take about six weeks to sprout shoots.

2 **Make holes** in the base of a large container, such as a garbage can or a large mesh sack. Add some crock, gravel, or stones, and fill the container with a 4 in (10 cm) layer of soil.

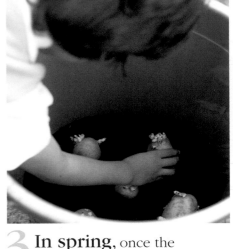

3 **In spring,** once the potatoes have sprouted short shoots, they are ready to plant. Carefully place five potatoes on top of the soil with the shoots facing upward.

5 **Once** the shoots reappear, cover them with more soil so that they are just buried. This is called "earthing up." Keep repeating this until the container is full.

6 **Keep the soil** well watered especially in dry weather. Remove any weeds. Use an all-purpose fertilizer every couple of weeks.

7 **Flowering shows** that the potatoes have reached a good size, so you can lift some out. Potatoes can be harvested as "new potatoes" in early summer.

Keep the potatoes well covered with soil by earthing up as they grow. They will turn green in sunlight. Green potatoes are poisonous.

The ancient Peruvians were the first to grow potatoes. Later, the Incas not only ate them, but also measured time by how long it took to cook them.

4 **Add a little more soil** to cover the potatoes by a further 1 in (2.5 cm) layer.

8 **Otherwise wait** until the leaves die back in the fall. Now, tip over the container and enjoy finding the potatoes among the soil. Look carefully.

Cook it Mashed potato fishcakes

You'll need

10 oz (250 g) undyed smoked haddock

1 fresh bay leaf

1½ cups (300 ml) milk

unpeeled, boiled then mashed
1 lb (375 g) potatoes

chopped finely
8 spring onions

¾ cup (100g) corn kernels

hand-boiled
4 eggs

chopped
2 tbsp fresh parsley

zest of 1 lemon

8 tbsp heavy cream

2 egg yolks

3 tbsp flour

1 tbsp (25 g) butter

a pinch of freshly ground black pepper

2 tbsp olive oil

7 cups (500 g) fresh shelled or frozen peas

a few spoonfuls of mayonnaise

4 tbsp yogurt or heavy cream

handful of cherry tomatoes

Baked, boiled, mashed, sliced and fried, or roasted, these are just a few of the many ideas for cooking your potatoes. They are a healthy energy-providing food. All you have to decide is which way will you cook them today.

Simmering time 5-10 mins

1 **Cook the haddock** fillets with the bay leaf and the milk in a shallow pan. Cool, then remove the fish's skin and any bones, and flake into chunks.

2 **Mix the fish,** potato, spring onions, corn kernels, eggs, parsley, and zest. In a small bowl, stir the cream with the egg yolks, and stir into the mixture.

3 **Divide** the mixture into four parts. With floured hands, shape each part into a slightly flattened ball. Roll each fishcake in the flour on a plate. Shaking off any excess.

4 **Heat the oil** and butter in a frying pan and carefully put in the fishcakes. Gently cook them for about 4-5 minutes on each side, or until golden brown.

Cooking time 2-3 mins

5 **To cook the peas,** bring a pan of water to the boil, then add the peas. Once cooked, drain away the water, using a strainer.

Go to page 78 for more potato recipe ideas

Serve with a spoonful of mayonnaise and halves of tomatoes.

Baked potato mice

6 **Place the peas** in a food processor and blend until smooth. Scrape the mashed peas into a bowl and stir in the yogurt or cream. Season with black pepper.

Onion

Plants from the onion family all have swollen leaf bases or bulbs. Large onions, spring onions, shallots, leeks, and even garlic are part of this family.

Onions can be grown more quickly by planting onion sets.

1 **Make a trench** ½ in (1.5 cm) deep in a small container. Sow onion seeds very thinly along the row. Cover with soil, then water, and add a label.

2 **Or, you could** sow your seeds in biodegradable bags. Sow your seeds in early spring or late summer for harvesting later in the year.

3 **After they have** germinated, thin out the onion seedlings and pull out any weeds. Keep the soil moist, but not very wet.

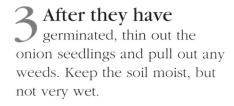

4 **Carefully transfer** your onions to a larger pot, spacing them out well. Water when the soil is dry and use a liquid plant food once a month.

5 **Pull back the soil** around the swollen onion bulbs. Break off any flower stems that appear and stop watering when the bulbs begin to ripen.

6 **Lift your onions** out of the ground two weeks after the leaves turn yellow and flop over. You might need to use a garden fork.

Leek
Grown for more than 6,000 years, leeks were even eaten by the ancient Egyptians, who built the pyramids.

Grow your own garlic
Place one clove, pointed end up, 2 in (5 cm) deep in a medium-sized pot and cover with a little soil. Always keep the soil moist. Break off all flower stems and stop watering in late summer. Lift in the same way as onions.

1 Make a hole ½ in (1.5 cm) deep in the soil with your finger or a pencil, and put in a few leek seeds. Cover with soil and water. You can keep the pots outdoors.

2 Once the seedlings are growing well, water them well. Then make some holes 6 in (15 cm) deep in a large pot. Now, lift out the seedlings and carefully separate them.

3 Trim each leek's root ends to 1 in (2.5 cm) long with scissors. Then place each one into its own hole in the large pot.

4 Fill each hole with water. The soil washed in will hold each leek in place. Continue to water regularly and use a liquid plant food once a month.

5 Get longer leeks by adding more soil to the pot, so raising the soil level around the base of each leek.

6 Lift some baby leeks when small. Other leeks you can leave in longer, even over winter, to grow bigger.

Cook it Onion and leek soup

Onions and leeks are great for adding flavor to savory meals. They also contain vitamins and minerals that will keep your hearts healthy.

You'll need

washed well

or vegetable stock

2 oz (50 g) butter	4 leeks, trimmed and sliced	1 large onion, chopped	2 medium potatoes, chopped	4 cups (1 liter) chicken stock	small bunch of tarragon, chopped	1 cup (250 ml) milk	salt and pepper	crème fraiche

Another recipe idea

Your eyes may water when peeling onions.

Onion pizza: see page 78

When fully grown, leeks need to be washed well to loosen any dirt between the leaves.

1 Melt the butter in a large saucepan, then add the onion and leeks. Cook gently for about 5-7 minutes until the onion and leeks are softened.

2 Add the potatoes and stock. Cook for a further 10 minutes or until the potatoes are tender.

3 Stir in the tarragon. Remove from heat and leave to cool. It is dangerous to blend a soup when hot, since the heat will force off the blender lid.

4 Pour the cold mixture into a blender. Blend until smooth. Reheat this soup with the milk in a saucepan. Season with salt and pepper.

5 **Serve the soup** in small bowls. Create a face with some crème fraiche on the surface of each soup. Serve with slices of bread if you wish.

A warm, tasty soup for cold winter days.

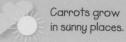
Carrots

Pulling up carrots is always a big surprise, because you won't know beforehand how big they'll be. The secret is to encourage good root growth, because this is the part we eat. There are many varieties and some take longer to grow than others.

1 Fill a very deep container with potting soil to give room for the long roots. Sow carrots where they are to grow, since they don't like being transplanted.

2 Sow seeds into a trench ½ in (1.5 cm) deep. Use your fingertips to cover the seeds with soil, then water and label. Keep outside from midspring.

3 Thin the germinated seedlings so that they are 3 in (8 cm) apart. You can use these thinnings in salads or put them into your compost bin.

4 Water often so the roots don't split. But be careful not to overwater, otherwise too much leaf will grow instead of the roots.

5 Lift some plants when small as baby carrots. Water before lifting so the other carrots are not disturbed.

6 Leave other carrots to get bigger and then pull up from the base of the stem. Use a garden fork to loosen the surrounding soil.

The first carrots were white, purple, red, yellow, green, or black. Long, orange carrots were developed in the 1500s by Dutch growers in honor of their royal family—the House of Orange.

Carrot pests can attack both the leaves and the roots of the plant.

Yuck, that leek stinks!

Companion planting

Sow leeks in with carrots. As they grow, they both have strong scents and may drive away each other's pests. This is called companion planting.

Cook it Carrot and orange muffins

You'll need

Preheat 400°F, 200°C	1 cup (140 g) all-purpose flour	½ cup (85 g) light brown sugar	⅓ cup (100 g) grated carrot	¾ cup (100 g) oats	½ tsp ground cinnamon	1 cup (200 ml) buttermilk	3 tbsp melted butter	2 tsp baking powder / ½ tsp baking soda

Muffin topping

2 oz (50 g) chopped roasted hazelnuts	½ cup (100 g) chopped finely unsulfered apricots	1 tbsp poppy seeds	zest of 2 oranges	1 egg, beaten	juice of 1 large orange	2 pinches of salt	2 tbsp soft brown sugar	1 tbsp melted butter	⅓ cup (50 g) oats

Carrots can be used in making both savory meals or sweet muffins. Full of healthy goodness and vitamins, these delicious muffins are ideal for a party or a treat for your lunchbox.

1 To make the topping, mix together the sugar, oats, and melted butter. Sprinkle the mixture onto a cookie sheet. Bake for five minutes, then leave to cool.

2 Mix the flour, baking powder, baking soda, and sugar. Add the nuts, carrot, apricots, poppy seeds, cinnamon, oats, and orange zest. Mix well.

3 In another bowl, use a spoon to mix the buttermilk, egg, butter, salt, and orange juice. Pour this onto the dry mixture.

4 Stir the two mixtures together using a spoon. Do not overmix as this will "knock out" all the air. The lumpier the mixture, the better the muffins will be!

5 Place eight muffin liners into a muffin pan. Spoon the mixture into the liners, filling them two-thirds full.

6 **Sprinkle the crumbly** topping over the muffins. Bake them for about 25-30 minutes until well risen and golden. Leave to cool.

A perfect lunchbox treat!

Go to page 78 for another carrot recipe idea.

Spinach

All parts of the plants from the spinach family have been cooked or used in medicines since ancient times. The tasty leaves and nutritious leafstalks can keep us healthy and strong.

5 Pick some outer leaves when longer than 2 in (5 cm). Encourage new growth by regularly picking a few leaves at a time.

1 In a long, deep container, make a trench 1 in (2.5 cm) deep using a ruler. Sow spinach seeds thinly along the row. Sow from midspring.

2 Once germinated, thin the seedlings to 3 in (8 cm) apart and throw away the ones you have removed. Thin them again at a later stage if necessary.

3 Keep well watered and use a liquid plant food once a month. Add a nitrogen-rich fertilizer to the soil for added goodness.

4 Pinch out flowering shoots as they appear so that the plant can concentrate on producing good leaves.

Beets

There are white and yellow as well as red varieties of beet. Farmers grow sugar beets and then extract the sugar.

1 Make some holes
1 in (2.5 cm) deep, spaced out around your large container. Sow two seeds into each hole. Cover with soil, water well, and put in a label.

2 Thin the germinated
seedlings when 1 in (2.5 cm) high to one per hole. Throw away the seedlings that you have removed.

Twist off the tops using your hands. (Don't cut with a knife or the beet will "bleed.") These leaves can be cooked and eaten just like spinach.

Do not grow the plants too close together or the roots will not grow very big.

3 Keep well watered
since dry spells can cause the beets to become woody and split, and stunt their growth.

4 Beets are ready
to pick when they are the size of golf balls. Lift the beet, holding the tops and using a fork to lever under the root.

Allow some others to grow bigger to the size of a tennis ball.

49

Here's a recipe to strengthen your muscles, boost your energy, and keep you healthy, all thanks to the minerals and vitamins in spinach.

Preheat

375°F.
190°C

For the pastry

| 1½ cups (150 g) whole-wheat flour | 1 cup (100 g) all-purpose flour | 5 oz (125 g) butter | 3 tbsp cold water | a pinch of salt | 1¾ lb (750 g) fresh spinach, trimmed | 2 egg yolks | 1 cup (200 ml) crème fraiche | nutmeg 1 clove garlic, crushed | freshly ground black pepper | freshly grated 2 oz (50 g) Parmesan |

1 Rub the butter into the flour until it is fine and crumbly. Stir in the salt and add enough water to bring the mixture together into a ball. Roll out the pastry thinly.

Baking time: 10 mins with beans and 5 mins without

2 Cut out 24 circles and press into muffin pans. Place a piece of parchment paper into each pastry and fill with baking beans. Bake in the oven.

Cooking time: 1–2 mins

3 Wash the spinach well then place in a large saucepan. Cover and cook until wilted, stirring once or twice. Wash under cold water until cool.

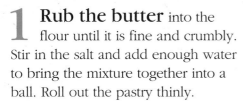

4 Drain well, then squeeze the spinach in a clean dish towel until as dry as possible. Chop roughly.

5 In a bowl, beat the egg with the crème fraiche and garlic. Season with freshly grated nutmeg and pepper and stir in the spinach.

Baking time: 15–20 mins

6 Spoon out the mixture evenly into the pastry shells. Sprinkle the Parmesan over the top of each tart. Bake in the oven until the filling has just set.

Plants protect themselves from pests by producing phytochemicals (fight-o-chemicals). When we eat them, the phytochemicals fight to keep us healthy, too. Spinach contains one called lutein, which keeps our eyes healthy.

Go to page 78 for another spinach recipe idea.

Grow lettuce in a sunny or slightly shaded place.

Lettuce
Flat or curly, green or purple—there are many varieties of crispy lettuce leaves. Sow the seeds at any time through the spring and summer, and end up with a long-lasting crop.

This funky lettuce is called Lollo Rosso.

1 **In a pot full** of potting soil, use a pencil to make a ½ in (1.5 cm) deep circular trench.

2 **Take a pinch** of the tiny seeds from a pile in your hand and sprinkle them along the trench.

3 **Cover the seeds** with soil, using your fingertips, then water the soil. Remember to label your pot with the variety of lettuce you have planted.

4 **Watch and wait** for the seedlings to grow. Pull out some seedlings to allow others to grow. Once a good size, transplant each lettuce into its own pot.

5 **Put your pots** on a high shelf and pour some gravel around the base of the lettuce to keep slugs and snails from getting to the leaves.

6 **Water often** to keep the soil moist. This needs to be done once or twice a day during warm weather, since the soil will dry out quickly.

Try using an old wooden crate for your crops. Line the crate with a waterproof plastic sheet, like a large garbage bag, and fill with potting soil. Sow the seeds directly into the soil. The wood keeps in valuable warmth and moisture.

Mix your seeds for a colorful crop.

Pick the outer leaves as you need them, and your lettuce will keep growing more and more leaves for you.

Cook it Rainbow salad

Food is full of color, and this healthy salad with a tofu dressing will bring dynamic color to the dinner table. A serving bowl with blue in its pattern will complete the rainbow.

Recipe idea: see page 19

Bulgar wheat salad

You'll need

DRESSING

6 oz (125 g) tofu

2 tsp sesame oil

½ tbsp rice vinegar
1 tbsp soy sauce

1 tbsp honey

1 tbsp water

2 tbsp mint, chopped

salt and freshly ground black pepper

2 tbsp pumpkin seeds

1 tbsp sesame

CROUTONS

6 slices wholewheat bread

2 tbsp extra-virgin olive oil

Preheat
400°F,
200°C

SALAD

mixed salad leaves

2 tbsp extra-virgin olive oil

1 tbsp mustard seeds

4 cups (250 g) fresh peas

cut into strips
½ yellow, ½ orange peppers

12 cherry tomatoes, halved

very thin
2 carrots, 2 raw beets, cut in strips

8 baby corns, cut in half lengthwise

1 Cut shapes out of the bread, using cookie cutters. Brush the bread with olive oil and bake in the oven for about five minutes, until golden brown.

2 Place all the ingredients for the dressing in a blender. Blend until smooth. Season with salt and pepper according to your taste.

3 Put the mixed leaves in a colander and wash with water. Drain well. Make a large bed of the leaves in a colorful serving bowl.

4 Scatter the pepper strips, fresh peas, and tomato halves on top of the salad leaves.

54

5 **Heat the olive oil** in a large frying pan and add the mustard seeds. Once they start to pop add beet, carrot, and baby corn. Cook until just tender then pour them over the salad ingredients in the serving bowl. Drizzle the dressing over the salad.

Sprinkle over the seeds and serve with the croutons.

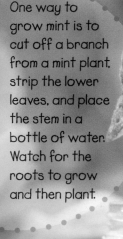

One way to grow mint is to cut off a branch from a mint plant, strip the lower leaves, and place the stem in a bottle of water. Watch for the roots to grow and then plant.

Mint

The leaves of a mint plant are great for flavoring food. You can grow mint from seed or a cutting from a friend's mint plant. This cutting method is called propagating.

1 **In fall or winter,** dig up part of a mint plant. Cut off a few good roots. Return the plant to its place.

2 **For each cutting,** make a straight cut where the root was attached to the parent plant. This is the top of the root.

4 **Fill a pot** with moist soil. Make some deep holes with a pencil. Place each root into a hole. The top end should be level with the surface of the soil.

5 **Cover the surface** with grit to push the soil down. Do not water. Watch and wait for the new plants to grow.

Mint has a very strong scent, which is said to repel aphids and other pests. So, mint can be a companion plant.

3 Make a sloping cut
a short distance along the root. This is the bottom of the root.

6 Plant the mint
cuttings into their own pots once the plants have grown good roots. Water to keep the soil moist.

1 In early spring,
make some holes in the bottom of a container, such as a clear plastic egg carton. Fill the container with moist soil or compost. Sprinkle the mint seeds very thinly onto the surface of the soil.

2 Close the lid
of the plastic egg carton, or cover the container, to keep the seeds warm. During germination, keep the soil moist but not very wet.

4 Water often
during the summer to keep the soil moist. Mint will grow and spread quickly. The young, tender leaves are ready to pick and use.

3 Lift out
a section of the seedlings when they have germinated and plant them into a larger pot.

5 Pick the growing tip
so the plant will become bushy. These leaves can be used for cooking. The plant will die back in fall and regrow in the spring.

Cook it Chocolate and mint mousse

You'll need

1¼ cups (300 ml) heavy cream

chopped

small bunch of mint

½ cup (125 ml) milk

small pieces

8 oz (175 g) dark chocolate

3 egg yolks

1½ tbsp confectioner's sugar

cocoa powder for dusting

Preheat
275°F.
150°C

Tickle your tastebuds with the flavor of mint. Throw a leaf or two into a pan of potatoes or peas, or into a glass of hot water for a refreshing tea, or into this mousse.

More mint recipes

Mint sauce: see page 79

Mint tea: see page 79

Why not make minty ice cubes by adding mint leaves to the water before freezing?

1 **Pour the cream** into a small pan. Add the chopped mint. Heat gently until nearly boiling, then remove from heat, cover, and leave for 30 minutes.

2 **Meanwhile,** pour the milk into another small pan and heat gently. Remove from heat and stir in the chocolate until it has melted and the mixture is smooth.

3 **Whisk the egg yolks** and sugar together and add the chocolate milk and the minty cream. Mix well, then strain the mixture through a fine strainer.

Baking time
45-60 mins

4 **Pour the mixture** into four ramekins or heat-proof cups. Stand the cups in a roasting pan. Add hot water until it's halfway up the outside of the cups. Bake.

Sooo chocolatey, sooo minty!

5 **While the mousse is** completely cooling in a refrigerator, make a stencil from a piece of cardboard. Cut out some different-sized holes in the cardboard. Before serving each chocolate mousse, hold the stencil over the top and sprinkle through some cocoa powder.

Sunflower

As bright as the Sun, these brilliant yellow flowers will stand out among your fruit and vegetables. But wait before picking, because it's the seeds you want to pick and eat.

Recycle newspapers by rolling them up to make biodegradable pots.

1 **At the end of spring,** put soil into some small pots with holes in their bases. Use your finger to make a hole 1 in (2.5 cm) deep in each pot.

2 **Sow one seed** into each hole. Cover the seeds lightly with soil. Water and place the pot onto a sunny windowsill.

3 **Cover the pot** with a see-through polyethylene bag to keep in the heat. Remove this bag when the leaves appear on the seedlings.

4 **Keep watering** little but often. Watch and wait. They'll be ready to plant outside when they are large enough to handle and their roots fill the pot.

5 **When a seedling** has outgrown its pot, it is ready to plant into a large container. Scoop out a pot-sized hole and carefully place the seedling into it. Water in.

6 **When the plant** is bigger, add a gardening pole a little way from the main stem. Use string to tie the stem to the pole. As it grows, make a tie every 8 in (20 cm).

Before opening, the flower bud will follow the position of the Sun through the day.

7 **Continue to water** little but often, since without water, the sunflower will quickly wither. Keep the plant free from pests by picking them off with your fingers.

8 **Use a measuring tape** to find out the height of your sunflower. You could make a chart to see how quickly it grows.

Wait for the flower heads to turn brown, then tap out the seeds.

Cook it Sunflowerpot loaves

Fill your kitchen with the homey smell of baking bread. Also, why not try roasting sunflower seeds to munch as a snack?

You'll need

 1¾ cups (250 g) white bread flour

 1¼ cups (150 g) whole-wheat flour

 1 tsp salt

 1 tsp sugar

 1 packet ½ oz (7 g) quick-rising yeast

 1 cup (250 ml) warm water

 2 tbsp extra-virgin olive oil

1 cup (100 g) sunflower seeds

four 5 x 4 in (11 x 10 cm) terra-cotta pots

a little milk

Preheat 400°F, 200°C

Baking time 35–40 mins

1 Scrub the new flowerpots with clean water. Oil the pots inside and out and bake them in a preheated oven. Let them cool. Repeat this process twice more.

2 Place the flour, salt, sugar, and yeast into a large bowl. Make a well in the center and pour in the water and olive oil. Mix to make a soft but firm dough.

3 Turn the dough out onto a lightly dusted work surface and knead well for at least 10 minutes. Get an adult to take a turn if your arms get tired.

4 Make a dip and add three-quarters of the sunflower seeds. Knead them into the dough.

You can leave the dough to rise overnight in the fridge.

5 Divide the dough into four pieces and place one ball into each flowerpot. Cover the pots with a plastic shopping bag and leave until the dough has doubled in size.

Cooking time 35–40 mins

6 Brush the tops of the risen loaves with a little milk. Sprinkle over the remaining sunflower seeds and bake the loaves in the oven until golden.

Go to page 79 for another sunflower seed recipe idea.

Slip me out of the pot and look what you've got!

63

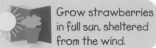
Grow strawberries in full sun, sheltered from the wind.

Strawberries

Follow the steps below and you will have delicious red strawberries to enjoy eating in the summer, year after year.

You can buy strawberry plugs from most garden centers or a mail-order supplier, who will send them in a box.

1 The easiest way to grow strawberry plants is to start off with strawberry plugs. The neat root ball makes the plugs easy to plant and quick to get growing.

2 Place the plug into a hole in a medium-sized pot. The top of the roots, called the "crown," should be level with the top of the soil. Water the soil well.

3 Put straw under the plant to stop the strawberries from lying on the ground. This also keeps the soil warm and stops the plant from losing moisture.

4 Water young plants every day. Once the plant is flowering, feed every 10 days until the strawberries are ready to pick.

Make more plants

Strawberry plants form runners during the growing season. In late summer, when the new plants along the runners have some roots, cut them from the parent plant. Leave about 2 in (5 cm) of runner each side of the new plants.

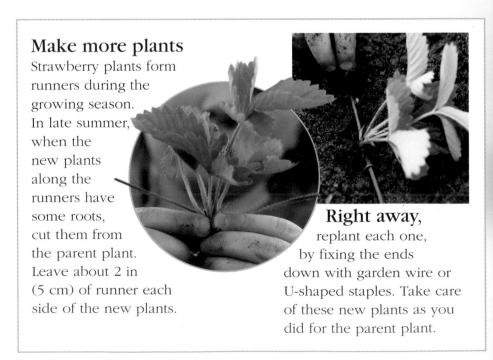

Right away, replant each one, by fixing the ends down with garden wire or U-shaped staples. Take care of these new plants as you did for the parent plant.

5 Check every other day to see if any strawberries have turned red. As soon as one is ripe, pick it right away, so that it doesn't rot. Make sure the green stalk stays on until the strawberry is eaten.

A strawberry is not really a fruit but the swollen base of the flower. There are about 200 seeds on the outer skin of each strawberry.

You may also want to cover your plant with netting to stop the birds from eating the strawberries.

Water often as the strawberries begin to swell.

Place the pot on a table, or put broken eggshells or grit under each plant to stop slugs from getting to them.

Cook it Strawberry meringue

Add color and flavor to cakes and desserts with your fresh and juicy-red strawberries. Sliced, blended, or eaten whole, they'll go down a treat.

You'll need

 3 egg whites

 a pinch of salt

 ½ cup (100 g) superfine sugar

 1oz (25 g) dark chocolate

 1 lb (500 g) fresh strawberries

 1 tbsp confectioner's sugar

1 cup (250 ml) whipping cream

Preheat 250°F, 120°C

1 Pour the egg whites and salt into a bowl and whisk until stiff and soft peaks form. Mix in the superfine sugar a spoonful at a time to make the meringue mixture.

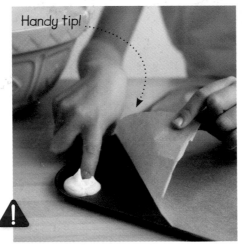

Handy tip!

2 Place a dollop of meringue mixture at each corner of a cookie sheet and place a piece of parchment paper on top. This will keep the parchment in place.

3 Melt the chocolate in a heat-proof bowl set over a saucepan of simmering water. Dribble a few spoonfuls of the melted chocolate over the mixture.

Cooking time 4 hrs

4 Scoop large spoonfuls of the swirly meringue onto the cookie sheet. Keep dribbling more chocolate into the bowl. Put the filled sheet into the oven.

Whizz till smooooooth!

5 Make the sauce while the meringues are cooling on a wire rack. Do this by placing half the strawberries and the confectioner's sugar into a blender and whizzing.

6 Whip the cream until soft, using a whisk. To serve, place a meringue on a plate and ladle a spoonful of cream over the top . . .

7... **Scatter over a** handful of sliced strawberries and then pour over the strawberry sauce, using a spoon. Now enjoy!

Top tip: For a low-sugar strawberry sauce, replace the confectioner's sugar with honey.

More strawberry recipes

Strawberry mousse: see page 79

Strawberry crepes: see page 79

Strawberry fondue: see page 79

Pick and eat!
You don't have to wait to taste your strawberries. Wash them and you can try them right away.

Blueberries

Blueberry bushes grow well in pots filled with acidic soil or soil mixed with peat. Care for them year after year and you'll be rewarded with lots of fruit.

How to begin?

You can either buy a young blueberry plant or one already brimming with fruit or flowers. If you plant two or more together, 3 ft (1 m) apart, then you'll get better fruit year after year.

3 ft (1 m)

In pots, blueberry bushes grow best filled with a mixture of potting soil and peat.

1 Fill your large pot with compost and soil mixture. Make a large hole and carefully drop in your blueberry plant. Add some more soil around the plant. Press down to make it stand firm.

2 Mulch around the new plant using bark or pine needles, which are fairly acidic. Do this again each spring.

3 Cover with netting, if your new plant already has some berries. This will stop the birds from eating the berries.

4 Water the new plant in well using rainwater. (Tap water will make the soil less acidic.) Continue to water your plant often from spring to fall.

Blueberries form on branches that grew in the previous year. To get the best berries, plants over three years old must be pruned each year, sometime between winter and spring.

Before pruning

After pruning

When pruning, remove any dead or diseased branches and cut off at the base one or two of the oldest branches that aren't producing much. This will make room for the younger branches and give you a good crop next time.

Blueberries form in clusters, but ripen at different times. Pick each berry a few days after it turns a deep blue color and easily pulls away.

Cook it Blueberry cheesecake

By the end of the summer, your blueberries will be ripe for the picking. Try eating them fresh with cream or yogurt, or add them to muffin mixes or smoothies.

You'll need

1 lb (500 g) blueberries	2 tbsp super-fine sugar	8 oz (250 g) cream cheese	1 cup (200 ml) crème fraîche	¼ tsp vanilla extract	8 oat cookies, crushed

More blueberry recipes

Pancakes: see page 79

Smoothie: see page 79

Muffins: see page 79

1 **Place ¾ of the berries** and ½ of the sugar into a small saucepan. Cover and simmer for five minutes until soft. Stir in the other berries and leave to cool.

2 **Using a wooden spoon,** beat the cream cheese, crème fraîche, remaining sugar, and vanilla extract together in a mixing bowl. Continue until well mixed and soft.

3 **Fill four glasses** with a spoonful of the blueberry sauce, then a spoonful of the cream cheese mixture, and then a spoonful of crushed cookies.

4 **Repeat the layers** once more and then put the filled glasses in the fridge for an hour.

Go to page 79 for more blueberry recipe ideas.

The blueberry is one of the few fruits native to North America. Some native Americans call it a star berry because the white flowers are shaped like five- pointed stars.

71

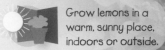
Lemon

All year round care for your lemon tree will reward you with a healthy, pretty tree with lots of lemons. Cover your tree in winter to protect it from frost and give it special food every month from early spring to late summer.

Growing from seed

As long as a lemon seed has not been damaged, it could grow into a lemon tree.

Select the seeds that are whole and undamaged. Sow them while they are still moist.

Cut a lemon in half and remove the seeds.

Lemon seed

Have patience! It's likely to take eight years or more before your plants flower and bear fruit.

Growing from a young tree

1 **Buy a lemon tree** that is ready to begin fruiting. Place it upright in a pot filled with citrus compost and soil. Add more soil if needed to help the tree stand firm.

2 **Add 2 in (5 cm) mulch** around the trunk to keep in moisture and warmth. Newly planted trees need to be watered often in the beginning.

3 **As the tree grows,** water very well only when the topsoil looks dry. During the winter, the tree will need less watering.

Lemons contain the most vitamin C of any citrus fruit. In the past, sailors ate them on voyages to stay healthy and quench their thirst.

From flower to fruit

Watch out for the lemon tree's sharp thorns!

The first flower buds will begin appearing in late spring.

Brilliant white flowers open to attract insects, such as bees, to take pollen from one flower to another.

Fruits form from pollinated flowers, turning from green to yellow as they swell.

73

Cook it Lemonade ice-pops

Keep cool on a hot summer's day with the zingy taste of your juicy lemons. Lemons add flavor to fish and salads as well.

Add slices of lemon to drinks and salads.

You'll need

18 ice-pop sticks

6 juicy lemons | 1 cup (250 ml) honey | 3 cups (700 ml) cold water | 18 yogurt cups

1 Finely grate the zest from three of the lemons and place in a pan with the honey and 2 cups (500 ml) water. Bring to the boil, then remove from heat.

2 Squeeze the juice from all of the lemons. Pour into a pitcher. This should give you about 1 cup (200-250 ml) of juice.

3 Strain the honey and lemon water through a strainer into a bowl. Pour in some of the lemon juice. Stir and taste. Add more juice until it tastes right.

Freezing time 1-2 hours

4 Leave the lemonade to cool in the fridge. Add the rest of the water to dilute. Stir, then pour into 18 empty yogurt cups. Place in the freezer until partly set.

5 Push an ice-pop stick into each cup. Return the cups to the freezer for another 1-2 hours until the lemonade becomes completely solid.

6 Crunch! Enjoy the cold juicy taste, but be quick, since your ice-pop will quickly start to melt on a warm day.

More lemon recipes

Lemon sorbet: see page 79
Scoop out a lemon
and use the skin as
a clever cup for
a lemon sorbet.

Throw in some ice cubes.
Sooo cool!

For a refreshing
drink, pour a little of your
lemonade (from Step 3)
into a glass and add some
cold soda water.

Many of the plants you have grown have produced seeds, which you could collect and then use next year. The secret of success is to collect the seeds at the right time and store them in the right way.

Sunflower seeds can be collected when the seed heads look big, fat, and brown. Cut off the whole seed head, put into a paper bag, and shake or pinch out the seeds.

Brilliant, bargain beans

1 Choose a healthy plant. Wait until the seed heads or seedpods have ripened and are about to split. Then, on a dry, windless day, cut off the entire seed head or pod.

store seeds in a paper bag

2 Remove the seeds using your fingers. In a warm place, leave the seeds to dry on a piece of kitchen towel. Label and store the seeds in a dry, cool place until spring.

3 Prepare a pot ready for sowing your seeds. Some seeds that are very dried out may need to be soaked first to encourage them to swell and germinate.

4 Last year's seeds have become this year's new plant. Why not trade seeds with other gardeners and give some to your friends to plant, too?

Make a seed box organizer

Your seeds need to be looked after while they are stored, so what better way to keep them cool, dry, and safe than in your own seed box. If carefully organized, you'll know when to sow the seeds next year at a glance.

SUMMER

Su SPRING

beans

zucchini seeds

1 **Find a box** and a lid and wrap them in colorful paper. Cut out some season dividers from cardboard.

2 **Paint a colorful design** on the dividers. When dry, write SPRING, SUMMER, and FALL on them to show when to sow the seeds next year.

3 **Decorate small envelopes** using colorful paints. Also, you could draw or stick on your own plant pictures. Once the envelope is dry, put the seeds inside.

Dwarf
french beans

Collected on
14th August 2007

Sow in spring

4 **Seal the envelopes** and label them with the name of the fruit or vegetable, its variety, and the date. Place in the organizer and cover with the lid.

Tomato sauce

Warm the oil in a large pan over a moderate heat. Add the onion and garlic, cover, and cook for about four minutes until the mixture is soft but not browned. Add the tomatoes, reduce the heat, cover, and cook for about 15 minutes until the tomatoes have collapsed. Remove from heat. Cool, then puree the mixture in a food processor or blender. Pass through a strainer. Use on pizzas or reheat before serving.

- 1 tbsp olive oil
- 1 small onion, finely chopped
- 1 garlic clove, finely chopped
- 2 lb (1 kg) whole ripe tomatoes

Ratatouille

Sprinkle salt over the eggplant and zucchini slices in a bowl; press down with a plate, and leave for one hour. Plunge the tomatoes in a bowl of boiling water for a few minutes, then skin them, quarter them, remove the seeds, and slice. Warm oil in a large pan. Fry onions and garlic for 10 minutes, then add peppers. Rinse the zucchinis and eggplants and dry with some paper towels. Add zucchinis, eggplants, and basil to the mixture and season. Stir, cover, and then simmer for 30 minutes. Add tomato flesh and cook for a further 15 minutes with the lid off. Use as a side dish or as a baked potato filling.

- 3 zucchinis, sliced
- 2 eggplants, sliced
- 2 onions, chopped
- 5 ripe tomatoes
- 2 red or green peppers, cored and chopped
- 2 garlic cloves, crushed
- 4 tbsp olive oil
- 1 tbsp basil
- salt and pepper

Stuffed zucchinis

Halve the zucchinis and blanch in boiling water for 3-4 minutes. Drain and cool. Scoop out seeds and a little flesh (to use later). Place zucchinis in a greased dish. Warm the oil in a small pan. Add onion and red pepper, cover, and cook until soft. Add garlic, thyme, zucchini flesh, and season with pepper. Stir the mixture and then spoon into the zucchini halves. Bake for 15 minutes.

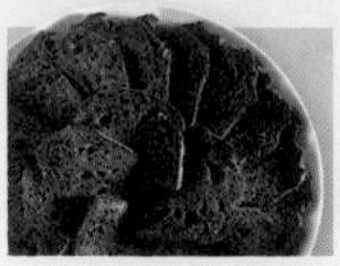

- 4 zucchinis
- 2 tbsp olive oil
- 1 onion, chopped
- 2 red peppers, cored and diced
- 2 garlic cloves, chopped
- 2 tbsp thyme
Preheat oven 350°F, 180°C

Pumpkin bread

Line a loaf pan with baking parchment. Sift the flour, baking powder, salt, cinnamon, and nutmeg into a bowl and make a hole in the middle. Mix the pumpkin, eggs, oil, and sugars. Pour ¾ of this mixture into the hole. Mix with a spoon, then stir in the remaining pumpkin mixture until smooth. Pour into the pan and bake for 55-60 minutes until the loaf begins to shrink from the sides. Cool slightly, then turn out onto a wire rack to cool completely.

- 1½ cups (180 g) all-purpose flour
- 1 tsp baking powder
- 1 tsp ground cinnamon
- ½ tsp salt
- ¼ tsp ground nutmeg
- 6 fl oz (180 ml) pumpkin puree (see p. 30)
- 2 eggs, beaten
- ¼ cup (60 ml) oil
- ½ cup (100 g) superfine sugar
- ¼ cup (50 g) brown sugar
Preheat oven 350°F, 180°C

Bean omelet

Heat the oil in a frying pan. Cook the onion, pepper, and beans gently until soft. Add the potato and cook for two minutes. Beat the eggs in a bowl. Stir in the onions, pepper, beans, and potatoes, and season with pepper. Melt the butter in a frying pan. Pour the mixture into the pan. Cook over a low heat for about 10 minutes, then cook the top under the broiler.

- 1 large onion, finely chopped
- 1 large red pepper, diced
- 1½ cups (150 g) green beans, chopped finely
- 2 medium cooked potatoes, sliced
- 2 tbsp olive oil
- 4 eggs
- 2 tbsp butter

Onion pizza

Boil the onions for six minutes; drain and cool. Thinly slice the onions. Sprinkle olive oil over the pizza crust, then spread the onions over it. Sprinkle on the cheese and herbs and season with salt and pepper. Bake in the oven for 25 minutes. Chop the parsley and sprinkle over the pizza. Serve.

- Pizza crust
- 3 medium onions
- 3 tbsp parsley
- 2 tbsp olive oil
- 1 oz (25 g) romano cheese
- 2 oz (50 g) mozzarella cheese
- 1 tsp mixed herbs
Preheat oven 425°F, 220°C

Baked potato mice

Wash potatoes and dry with paper towel. Prick with a fork and place on a cookie sheet. Cook for 60-75 minutes until the inside is soft and the skins crisp. Remove from oven. Cut each potato in half and scoop out the soft insides into a mixing bowl. Place the skins back on the cookie sheet. Mash the potato well, add butter and seasoning, and spoon back into the skins. Sprinkle the cheese over the potatoes and cook in the oven for a further 15 minutes. For each potato, press on two radish halves for the ears, chives for the whiskers, a tomato for the nose, raisins for the eyes, and a scallion for the tail.

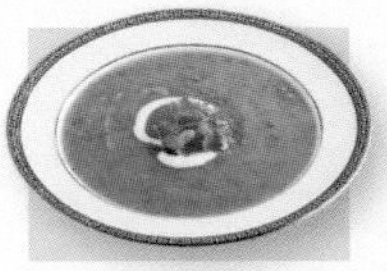

- 4 large potatoes
- 2 oz (50 g) butter
- salt and pepper
- 5 oz (125 g) Cheddar cheese, grated
- 4 radishes, halved
- 4 cherry tomatoes
- chives, chopped in sticks
- 8 raisins
- 2 scallions, halved
Preheat oven 400°F, 200°C

Carrot soup

Put the carrots, garlic, zest, orange juice, and water in a pan. Cover and simmer for 20 minutes until the carrots are soft. Let the soup cool, then add nutmeg and lemon juice. Pour into a blender and blend until smooth. Return the soup to the pan, stir in the cream, and season with pepper. Then reheat the soup without letting it boil.

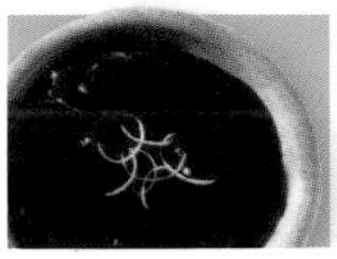

- 6 carrots, peeled and sliced
- 2 cloves garlic, peeled
- zest of 1 orange, grated
- juice of 1 lemon
- 1¼ cups (300 ml) water
- pinch of ground nutmeg
- 1¼ cups (300 ml) orange juice
- 1¼ cups (300 ml) light cream

Beet salad

Trim and scrub the beet, then place in a pan and cover with slightly salty water. Bring to a boil and cook the beet for about 30 minutes until a knife can pass through easily. Drain well and skin when cool enough to handle. Slice into pieces, sprinkle over the pieces of orange peel, and serve.

- homegrown beet
- a pinch of salt
- orange peel, sliced finely

Spinach gnocchi

To make the sauce, warm the oil in a frying pan. Add onion, carrot, and celery and cook for 10 minutes. Add the tomatoes, season, and simmer for 25-35 minutes, stirring occasionally until the sauce thickens. Pour into a blender and puree. To make the dough, boil the potatoes until tender, drain well, and then mash. Boil the spinach for two minutes, drain, and then chop finely. Mix the potatoes and the spinach with the flour to form a dough. Knead the dough on a floured board. Divide into 12 pieces and roll each piece into a long cylinder. Cut into ¾ in (2 cm) pieces to make gnocchi. Boil the pieces for two minutes, drain well, and place in a greased baking dish. Reheat the sauce, stir in the cream, season, and spoon over the gnocchi. Bake for 5-7 minutes. Garnish with parsley before serving.

For the dough:
- 1 lb (500 g) potatoes, peeled
- 5 cups (125 g) fresh spinach
- ¾ cup (75 g) all-purpose flour

For the sauce:
- 1 tbsp oil
- 1 small onion
- 1 small carrot
- 1 celery stick
- 5 tomatoes, peeled, deseeded, and chopped
- ½ cup (125 ml) heavy cream
- pepper to season
- sprigs of parsley, chopped

Preheat oven 425°F, 220°C

Bulgar wheat salad

Soak the bulgar wheat in a bowl of boiling water for 20 minutes until the grains soften. Drain the bulgar in a strainer over a bowl and squeeze out any extra water with your hands. Put all the ingredients in a bowl, mix together, and season with pepper. Arrange the washed lettuce leaves on a serving bowl and then pour the bulgar mixture on top.

- lettuce leaves
- 1½ cups (175 g) bulgar wheat
- ½ cucumber, finely chopped
- 4 scallions, finely sliced
- 1 bunch parsley, chopped
- handful of mint leaves, chopped
- 3 tbsp olive oil

Mint tea

Put tea and mint leaves in a teapot. Pour boiling water over the leaves. Let stand for three minutes. Strain the tea before serving. Serve with a leaf or two of mint and a slice of lemon. Sweeten with honey if needed.

For each cup:
- ½ tsp tea leaves
- ½ tsp crushed mint leaves
- 1 cup boiling water
- sprig of mint
- slice of lemon

Mint sauce

Place the mint and sugar into a pitcher and pour over the boiling water. Stir and leave to cool. Add vinegar and mix well. Add more water or vinegar and season to taste.

- Bunch of mint leaves, chopped finely
- 4 tbsp white wine vinegar
- 4 tbsp boiling water
- 1 tbsp superfine sugar

Sunflower salad

Peel and grate the carrot. Toast the sunflower seeds lightly under the broiler for a few minutes. Put the dressing ingredients into a jar, screw on a lid, and shake well. Put the carrot, sunflower seeds, and raisins into a salad bowl. Pour the dressing over the top. Toss the salad using two spoons. Season with salt and pepper if you wish.

- 6 large carrots,
- 1 tbsp sunflower seeds
- ½ cup (85 g) raisins

For the dressing:
- juice from ½ orange
- juice from ½ lemon
- 1 tsp honey
- 3 tbsp olive oil
- ¼ tsp French mustard

Crepes

Sift flour and salt into a bowl. Make a "well" in the center, add the egg and half the milk. Beat together and gradually mix in the flour until smooth. Beat in the rest of the milk and pour into a pitcher. Heat the pan over a medium heat. Add a teaspoon of butter or oil and swirl around. Pour two tablespoons of batter into pan, and tilt back and forth so the batter evenly coats the base. After 30 seconds, lift the edge of the crepe with a spatula to see if it is brown underneath. Loosen around the edges and flip the crepe. A few seconds later, slide the crepe out of the pan and onto a warm plate. Stack crepes between layers of parchment paper. Cover with foil to keep warm. Or, serve immediately and sprinkle some strawberry slices and a dollop of cream, and fold the crepe over.

For 10 crepes:
- 1 cup (100g) all-purpose flour
- pinch of salt
- 1 egg, beaten
- 1¼ cups (300 ml) milk
- 10 tsp butter or olive oil

For filling:
- strawberry slices and whipped cream

Alternative crepe filling:
- freshly squeezed lemon juice and superfine sugar

Alternative:
- Add ¼ cup (50 g) blueberries and
- 2 tbsp sugar into batter mixture.
To serve pour on maple syrup

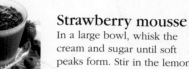

Strawberry mousse

In a large bowl, whisk the cream and sugar until soft peaks form. Stir in the lemon juice to thicken. Mash the strawberries, then fold in to the mixture. Spoon the mixture into four serving glasses.

- ¾ cup (100 g) strawberries
- 3 tbsp sugar
- 1 cup (220 ml) heavy cream
- juice of 1 lemon

Strawberry fondue

Put the cream and chocolate in a saucepan. Over a low heat, stir the mixture until the chocolate has melted. Pour into the fondue pot. Dip the strawberries into the pot using fondue forks.

- 8 oz (200 g) dark or milk chocolate
- ½ cup (80 ml) of heavy cream strawberries

Blueberry smoothie

Put all the ingredients into the blender. Add superfine sugar if required. Cover and blend until smooth. Pour into glasses and serve.

- 1 small banana
- 1 cup (150 g) blueberries
- 1½ cups (300 ml) milk

Blueberry muffins

Whisk the butter and sugar until fluffy. Still whisking, add the eggs one at a time. Add the vanilla extract and milk. Fold in the flour and a teaspoon of baking powder to make thick batter. Add the blueberries. Spoon the mixture into 12 paper muffin cases in a muffin pan. Bake for 30 minutes.

- ½ cup (100 g) superfine sugar
- 4 oz (100 g) butter
- 2¾ cups (300 g) flour
- 1 tsp baking powder
- 2 eggs, beaten
- 5 fl oz (140 ml) milk
- 1 tsp vanilla extract
- 1¼ cups (150 g) blueberries

Preheat oven 300°F, 160°C

Lemon sorbet

Cut the tops off four lemons; scoop out the flesh and place the rinds in the freezer. Put the lemon flesh, sugar, and water in a saucepan. Bring to the boil and simmer for five minutes. Strain the mixture and cool. Puree in a food processor until smooth. Scoop into the frozen lemon peels and freeze in an airtight container until ready to serve.

- 2¼ cups (400 g) sugar
- 1½ cups (300 ml) water
- 6 lemons

Index

Suppliers

DK would like to thank:

Delfand Nurseries Ltd.
Wholesale; Nursery shop;
Mail order suppliers.
Benwick Road, Doddington,
March, Cambs. PE15 0TU
Tel: +44 1354 740553
www.organicplants.co.uk

Garsons
Farm Shop; Pick Your Own.
Winterdown Road, West End,
Esher, Surrey, UK KT10 8LS
Address to go here
Tel: +44 1372 464389
www.garsons.co.uk

Roots and Shoots
Wild Garden; Study Centre
Walnut Tree Walk
London, UK SE11 6DN
Tel: +44 20 7587 1131
www.rootsandshoots.org.uk

The Garlic Farm
Newchurch, Isle of Wight, UK
Tel: +44 1983 865378
www.thegarlicfarm.co.uk

**Brockwell Park
Community Greenhouses**
Brixton, London

Antonia Salt at Green Ink
Garden Design Practice
www.greeninkgardens.com

Keift & Sons Ltd.
Quality flower bulbs
Tel: +44 1603 868911
www.kieftbulbs.co.uk

**Alleyn Park Garden
Centre Ltd.**
Rear of 77 Park Hall Road,
London, UK SE21 8ES
Tel: +44 20 8670 7788
www.alleynpark.co.uk

Acknowledgments

DK would like to thank:
Vauxhall City Farm
Urban farm; Community garden.
165 Tyers Street, London, UK
SE11 5HS Tel: +44 20 7582 4202
E-mail: vcf@btconnect.com
Director: Sharon Clouston
Community gardener:
Bernadette Kennedy

Staff and volunteers from VCF;
and Diane Sullock, responsible
for the community dye garden

With thanks to VCF for the use of their garden and for taking care of our plants.

DK Team
Sadie Thomas,
Deborah Lock,
Sonia Whillock-Moore

Photographer
Will Heap
www.willheap.com

Food Stylist
Annie Nichols
Annieisonthebeach Ltd.

Models: Stanley and Scarlet
Heap, Fiona Lock, Hannah
and Max Moore, Matthew
Morley, Jamie Chang-Leng,
Spencer Britton, Kitty Nallet,
Saphira Noor, Cara
Crosby-Irons, Alfred and
Molly Warren.

Picture credits

The publisher would like to thank the following for their kind permission to reproduce their photographs:

(Key: a-above; b-below/bottom; c-center; l-left; r-right; t-top)
Alamy Images: Blickwinkel/Schmidbauer 12c; Blickwinkel/tomcook 68bl, 68cl; Creon Co.Ltd 75tl, 77fbr; Tim Gainey 70ftl; Andrea Jones 7fcla; MShieldsPhotos 73l; **Corbis:** J. Hall/photocuisine 76cb; **Flickr.com:** 4cr, 6fcr, 7c; John Barnabus 6tr; Buena Vida 60cr; Elemmakil 72c; Vanessa Evans 52ftr; Jomp Agullet 60tr; Mearse 6cr; Ken B. Miller 72cra; Tweetie Bird 73tr; **GAP Photos:** Visions 69c; **Getty Images:** Visuals Unlimited/John Gerlach 68tl; **Photolibrary:** Juliette H. Wade/Espalier Media Ltd. 53tr; **Photoshot / NHPA:** Stephen Dalton 45cb; **PunchStock:** BananaStock 14cb; **Science Photo Library:** B. W. Hoffman/Agstockusa 10-11c.
Jacket images: *Front:* flickr.com: Totteboll t

All other images © Dorling Kindersley
For further information see: www.dkimages.com